SUMMER OF SERVICE

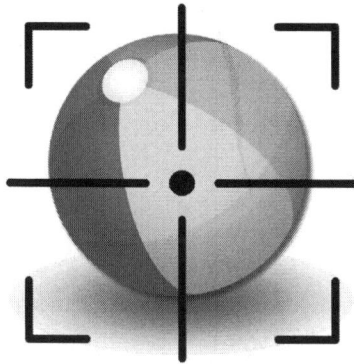

A HIGH SCHOOLER'S GUIDE TO SERVING, LEARNING, AND GROWING DURING SUMMER BREAK

COLE + MADDOX BAILEY

Publisher: Contact Buzz'd Books at hello@buzzdbooks.com if you're interested in quantity discounts for your company, school, children's organization, or scout troops for reselling, educational purposes, subscription incentives, gifts, or fundraising campaigns.

Book Cover Design and Illustrations: Canva

Book Layout Design: Atticus

ISBN (paperback): 979-8-9874504-5-1

ISBN (ebook): 979-8-9874504-6-8

This book is typeset in OpenDyslexic, a font designed by Abbie Gonzalez to reduce common reading errors experienced by people living with Dyslexia.

Contents

Chapter 1

Mission Possible

Greetings, change agent:

Your mission, should you choose to accept it, will challenge you, change you, and, most importantly, allow you to change the world around you. Be advised that your summer break won't be typical. This Summer of Service will propel you headfirst into the world of volunteering.

Before we dive into the blueprints of your summer capers, here's a bit about us, Cole and Maddox, the twin masterminds behind this operation.

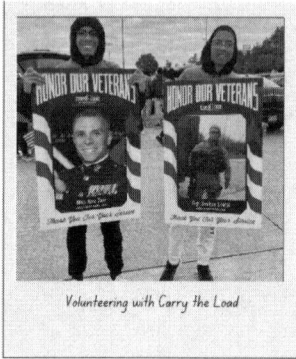
Volunteering with Carry the Load

We're the dynamic duo who jumped into the world of volunteering with the Young Men's Service League (YMSL)—a group of young change agents and their chief operatives (aka our moms) dedicated to community service and leadership development. Our mission began at home, where the art of giving back was as essential as our secret handshake. YMSL gave us the league, but it was our spirit of adventure that set the stage.

As twins, we're a package deal with a twist—think of us as different sides of the same coin. One of us thrives in the limelight, dodging physical labor like a pro, while the other prefers the shadows, finding strength in the sweat and work of hands-on missions.

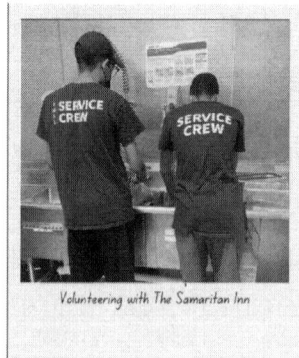
Volunteering with The Samaritan Inn

Our completed missions include:

- **Intel Gathering**: As summer counselors, we've cracked the code for boosting Dallas students' literacy rates.

- **Construction and Demolition**: On the front lines of the Texas Ramp Project, we built ramps for those in need.

- **Operative Care**: Providing essential services such as shower valets for the homeless with Streetside Showers.

- **Supply Drops**: Delivering food to seniors with Meals on Wheels.

- **Field Support**: Serving up hope (and meals) at the Community Garden Kitchen.

- **Eco-Warfare**: Battling the urban heat with Texas Trees Foundation, one tree at a time.

- **Morale Boosting**: Running carnival games for Rainbow Days **serving at-risk children and youth** because every child should have fun.

- **Respite Recon**: Serving as caregivers to families with special-needs kids a breather with Rays of Light.

- **Logistics**: Packing life-saving meals to be sent around the world with Feed My Starving Children.

- **Honor Guard**: Marching with Carry the Load to honor our veterans.

And that's just the tip of the iceberg. Each mission has been a step on our journey, a story in our book of adventures.

We think that once you start volunteering you'll keep coming back for some of the same reasons we do. The sense of community, the smiles you bring to people's faces, and the sheer joy of making a difference—it's addictive, in the best way possible. Not to mention, each new project is like unlocking a level in the most epic game ever, where the rewards are real-life achievements and personal growth. Plus, let's be honest, it's a fantastic way to rack up some awesome stories for college essays or chats with friends.

So, why not dive in? The more you volunteer, the more you realize that the world is a little bit brighter every time you lend a hand.

And this book is just the guide you need. Let us tell you a bit more about it. When word of our missions leaked onto Facebook (thanks to our mom), the response was overwhelming. The call to action became clear: answer the questions that we were getting over and over again. So we drafted a manual to help others do the same thing we were doing. In this manual, we're not just answering questions; we're equipping you to join the front lines of change.

Your objectives are clear: Identify a cause (or causes) that lights a fire in your heart, connect with a community in need, and deploy your unique skills to make a real impact. Local animal shelters are crying out for a hero, community gardens dream of greener futures, and many causes desperately need your help.

You will not be alone in this endeavor. Along the way, you'll join forces with fellow change agents—kind-hearted individuals who share your passion for service and determination to make a difference. Together, you'll form an unstoppable force of goodwill, compassion, and change.

Be warned: This mission is not for the faint of heart. You'll encounter challenges, unexpected hurdles, and even battle the occasional case of self-doubt. But don't worry. We got you. Within these pages lies your mission plan for success—a guide filled with secret tips, strategies, and stories to inspire your journey.

Remember, these summer volunteering adventures could change you for the better. Your impact could echo throughout your community and beyond, inspiring others to join your cause and continue spreading waves of positive transformation.

This message will self-inspire in five seconds. Your mission begins now. Welcome to your Summer of Service.

Chapter 2

Situation Room:

UNDERSTANDING THE MISSION AHEAD

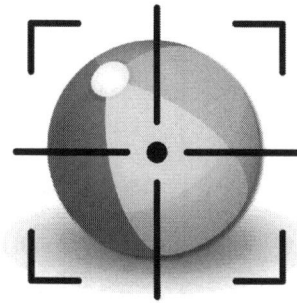

Welcome to the "Situation Room," change agent!

Picture this: a high-tech underground bunker, screens flickering with global crises, and the buzz of secret intel in hushed voices. This isn't just any room; it's the nerve center of our operations, where we strategize, plan, and launch our most covert missions.

But don't worry. You won't need to dodge lasers, crack complex codes, or use retina scanners to get through this door. Instead, you've been granted top-secret access to tackle something even more thrilling: mapping out your mission plan to become a volunteer change agent this summer. So grab your gadgets, cue the dramatic music, and suit up.

Think of this book as your gadget-filled briefcase, packed with inspiration for hundreds of missions designed to challenge, thrill, and, most importantly, change you.

Maybe you've heard of Phineas and Ferb. These cartoon hero stepbrothers turn every day of summer vacation into a new epic adventure. While most kids are chilling with video games or at the pool, Phineas and Ferb construct backyard roller coasters, portals to Mars, or climb up the Eiffel Tower—the usual suburban to-do list. You can channel your inner Phineas and Ferb creativity toward projects that will truly make a difference this summer. Things like safeguarding the planet to championing the underdog. This is your mission.

So, change agent, are you ready to accept your mission and embark on a summer of significance? To learn, grow, and perhaps alter a few destinies, including your own?

As we wrap up our initial briefing in the Situation Room, if this feels overwhelming, remember that this book contains a step-by-step guide designed to equip you with the skills and knowledge needed to navigate the heroic world of volunteering.

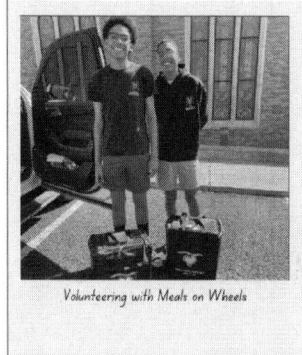

Volunteering with Meals on Wheels

Here's to a season of secret missions, where the rewards are measured in smiles, high fives, and hearts touched. From identifying your passions and connecting with impactful causes to launching into action and leaving a lasting mark on the world, we've got you covered. Think of each section as a vital component of your mission, laying the groundwork for the incredible adventures you're about to undertake.

So, tighten your utility belt, sharpen your focus, and prepare to transform both your community and yourself. Next up, we discuss some heroic inspiration and how volunteering can boost your own superpowers. Let's get into the mindset to make this summer one for the history books!

Chapter 3

Action With Impact:

BECOME A CHANGE AGENT THIS SUMMER

On paper, opting for gaming marathons and pocket-money gigs might seem like the ideal way to spend your summer vacation. But what if we told you that swapping a joystick for a shovel at a community garden could turbocharge your life?

The truth is, volunteering unlocks levels of awesomeness you never knew existed. We want to recruit you into the ranks of those who've discovered the secret: a few hours of giving back can unlock rewards that are both epic and unexpected. Trust us, the trade-off is a game-changer.

If you're still on the fence, let's look at an uplifting example from the world of superheroes.

Consider Captain America, a hero who transforms from a dedicated volunteer into a super-soldier. Before becoming Captain America, Steve Rogers repeatedly tried to enlist in the Army to serve his country. He's rejected for his small stature and various health issues.

Eventually, his persistence and desire to contribute positively to society catch the attention of Dr. Abraham Erskine, who ultimately selects Steve for the super-soldier experiment.

Once transformed, Steve doesn't use his powers for personal gain. Instead, he devotes himself to protecting the innocent and battling tyranny. He embodies the spirit of selfless service. His journey from a simple volunteer to a hero with superhuman abilities highlights how

the desire to help can lead to extraordinary personal growth as well as create a big impact.

Just like Captain America, your choice to volunteer this summer could set off a chain of positive events. By choosing to step up and serve, you not only enhance your own life but potentially inspire and uplift those around you. It's an example of how even small decisions, like where to dedicate your time and energy this summer, can have a profound impact on your personal development and the community.

Now, let's channel our inner change agent and see how volunteering can unleash our own set of superpowers.

Step Into New Worlds

Volunteering whisks you away into the lives of others, offering a real-life VR experience of their world. It's like flipping the switch from standard to HD—everything's more vibrant, more complex, and infinitely more interesting. Ever helped out at a shelter? It's an eye-opener to the stories behind the faces, breaking down stereotypes and building a web of understanding that spans the community. Imagine spending time in a park with no trees for shade—it gives you a real feel for the value of green spaces and why we need to protect them.

Skill Up, Level Up

Jumping into the action, you'll pick up an arsenal of skills—teamwork, quick thinking, leadership—like collecting power-ups in a game. These aren't just life skills; they're your advance tickets to future opportunities, whether in college, careers, or quests yet to unfold.

Be the Hero of Your Story

Every act of kindness, big or small, lights up the world a bit more. Helping someone conquer algebra, reviving a park, or sharing a meal can spark a chain reaction of positivity.

NOT ALL Heroes WEAR CAPES

You're not just earning karma points. You're actively crafting a brighter narrative for yourself and those around you.

Forge Alliances

The volunteering world is your community, where you'll meet allies with shared interests—from the people you're helping to fellow volunteers and the leaders making waves in the community. These aren't just acquaintances but potential lifelong partners, mentors, and friends.

Boost Your Hero Profile

Volunteering doesn't just feel good. The experiences you gain add some serious flair to your resume and college applications, showcasing you as a protagonist who's ready to step up and face any challenge.

As we wrap up this briefing, remember that volunteering isn't just an act of charity. This mission could transform your summer from ordinary to extraordinary.

Ready to unlock your hidden superpowers? Stay tuned for the next chapter, where we decode the mystery of turning volunteer experiences into resume gold and equip you for future success.

Chapter 4

Skill Arsenal:

EQUIPPING YOURSELF WITH VOLUNTEER EXPERIENCE

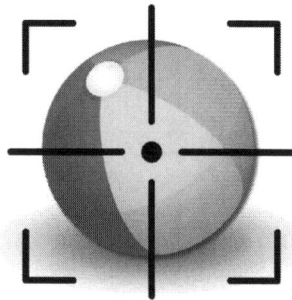

Something to keep in mind as you begin to plan your Summer of Service is the potential impact on your own life. Some people might feel awkward about volunteering to boost their resume experience, but the truth is it's a win-win situation.

Volunteering helps communities, causes, and non-profits that need it while giving volunteers the skills and experiences they need. It's the ultimate win-win! In this chapter, we explore how a Summer of Service can fuel personal growth and turbocharge your resume while making a difference.

Let's face it. Most high school students lack real-life experiences to set them apart in the sea of resumes.

At this stage in our lives, opportunities for formal employment or professional achievements are pretty slim. Most of us haven't had the chance to work in part-time jobs, internships, or other roles that build resumes. This lack of experience can make gauging a student's potential and capabilities challenging for admissions committees and employers.

Volunteering is one possible solution to this dilemma. It showcases a willingness to commit time and energy to causes you care about and provides evidence of your interests and skills. Employers and college admissions committees will view a resume that reflects compassion, initiative, and experience.

Leading a community event, collaborating on a service project, or navigating challenges in tough situations will showcase your capabilities. These experiences demonstrate your skills in ways that grades alone don't capture. They highlight the depth of your ability to lead, work as part of a team, and solve problems creatively.

In addition to showcasing your desirable personal qualities, volunteer experiences can hint at your career interests and potential majors, making college applications more compelling. For example, volunteering at a healthcare facility could indicate an interest in pursuing medicine, while involvement in environmental clean-ups could demonstrate a passion for environmental science.

This alignment between your volunteer experiences and academic or career aspirations can significantly strengthen your application. Real talk, it will set you apart from other candidates who may not have as clear a direction or demonstrated commitment to their fields of interest.

Unlock New Talents and Perspectives

Volunteering also exposes you to new challenges and situations you usually don't find in a school classroom setting. This hands-on experience can help you develop valuable life skills, such as teamwork, communication, problem-solving, and leadership.

Working with United to Learn taught us to write lesson plans, for example. When we built our first wheelchair ramp, we used power tools for the first time. And busing tables and serving meals at the Community Garden Kitchen gave us hands-on experience that could help us get a job at a restaurant one day.

Explore Your Interests

Volunteering is one of the most effective ways to gain hands-on experience for possible future careers while contributing positively to your community. It is an opportunity to explore a field meaningfully, and this hands-on experience can help you decide if a particular career you're considering is actually something you'd be interested in.

Thinking about a career in veterinary medicine? Volunteering at animal shelters can get you started. Interested in the buzz of business? Help with marketing for a non-profit. Dreaming of becoming a chef? Start in community kitchens. Volunteering puts you right in the action. It's more than just padding your resume—each role provides a real-world look at potential careers. These can range from healthcare and technology to environmental advocacy and the arts.

Want to explore a hospital from the inside, lead a classroom, or learn the basics of carpentry? There's a volunteering opportunity that fits your interests. It will also broaden your horizons and test your skills in a

Volunteering with Texas Ramp Project

real-world setting. As you dive into these experiences, you'll discover new interests and might even find your dream job. So why wait? Start exploring

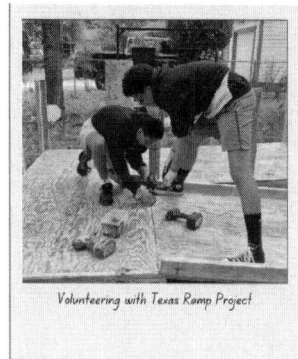

and shaping your future, one volunteer gig at a time.

The Best Perk of All: Fun

We've already talked about how volunteering has some serious perks, from feeling awesome about making a difference in someone's life to gaining experiences and skills that no classroom or job can teach you. The truth is that it can actually be fun. You meet new people who care about the same stuff you do and get to do things you'd never thought you'd try.

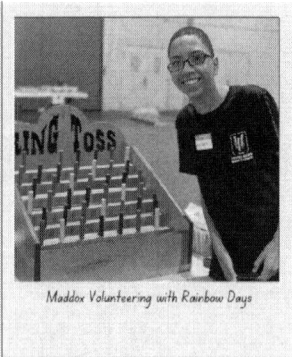
Maddox Volunteering with Rainbow Days

Imagine spending a Saturday building a playground—sure, it's work, but it's also a blast to play around with tools and see something you built used by kids at the end of the day. Or think about joining a beach clean-up, where you may end up having an impromptu sandcastle competition. It's these unexpected moments that make volunteering not just worthwhile but genuinely enjoyable.

Plus, the camaraderie that comes with working alongside others who are there because they want to be, not because they have to be, creates a unique bond. You'll find yourself making friends in no time, laughing over

Cole Volunteering with Rainbow Days

shared tasks, or cheering each other on as you tackle new challenges together. Whether you're painting murals, planting gardens, or walking dogs at the animal shelter, each activity gives you a chance to lighten up and have some fun while doing good.

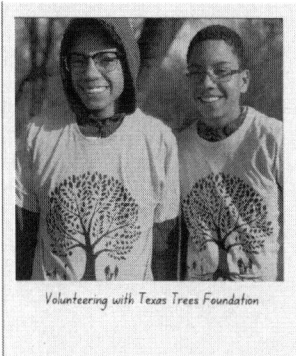
Volunteering with Texas Trees Foundation

So, don't just sit there wondering what volunteering might be like—jump in and experience the fun firsthand. Who knows? It could turn into your new favorite hobby, all while you contribute to a bigger cause. It's about making memories, making friends, and making a difference—all rolled into one. What's not to love about that?

With all this in mind, are you ready to make your mark in the world of volunteering, build up your skill arsenal, and have some fun? That's where our next chapter, "Field Guide: The G.I.V.E. Framework," comes in handy. If you're pumped to get going but still figuring out where to start, don't sweat it—we're here to streamline the process for you. Think of G.I.V.E. as your personal compass to find your direction in the ocean of volunteer opportunities. No need to feel overwhelmed. We're here to make your volunteer journey as impactful and enjoyable as possible.

So, flip that page, and let's get into the nitty-gritty of the framework that will set the stage for your summer volunteer adventure.

Chapter 5

Field Guide:

THE G.I.V.E. FRAMEWORK

If you've stuck with us this far, it's pretty clear you're ready to roll up your sleeves and make a difference. And let's be real, that's pretty epic. With the world being as vast and varied as it is, picking where to lend a hand might seem like finding a needle in a haystack. But no stress, we've got your back.

There is a simple way to start your volunteer journey. All you have to remember is G.I.V.E., and you'll be good to go.

Here's what G.I.V.E. stands for:

G–Great Cause

I–Internet

V–Volunteer

E–Enjoy, Engage, and Expand

G.I.V.E. is your golden ticket to kicking off your volunteer adventure without the headache of sifting through a million options. Let's break it down a bit more, shall we?

G—Great Cause: This is all about finding that spark. What lights you up? Is it protecting the environment, helping animals, or supporting people in need? Think about what gets you fired up and start there. Your passion is your compass.

I—Internet: In this step, you put on your detective hat and do a little digging. You can research organizations that align with your chosen cause with an internet search. Look into what they do, who they help, and how they do it. This step ensures that your time and energy go to a place that really speaks to you and is a legit non-profit. More on that later.

V—Volunteer: You've picked your cause, done your homework, and now it's showtime. Get out there and volunteer (more information to come). Whether it's a one-time event or a regular gig, your contribution is about to make waves. Remember, every little bit helps.

E—Enjoy, Engage, and Expand: This is the secret sauce. Volunteering isn't just about giving; it's also about what you get in return. Enjoy the process, engage fully with the experience, and watch your world expand. As we've discussed, you'll meet new people, learn new things, and maybe even discover new sides of yourself.

By following the G.I.V.E. roadmap, you're not just signing up for volunteer work; you're taking an adventure. An adventure that promises growth, connections, and the unmatched joy of contributing to a cause you believe in.

While we briefly introduce the G.I.V.E. framework, we'll explore each step in more detail so you can fully grasp how each component enhances your volunteering adventure.

In the next chapter, we will start with "G" (Great Cause), hoping that at least one of those discussed will resonate with you. This list doesn't capture every possibility because that's impossible, but the broad categories are still helpful.

So, if you're ready to find your volunteering match, turn that page, and let's start discovering causes that can change your life.

Chapter 6

"G," Great Cause:

RECON FOR THE HEART

Assessing Your Agent Profile

In this chapter, we explore some incredible causes, each one eager for a hero like you to step in and make a mark. Remember, the causes we're about to discuss are just the tip of the iceberg. The world is full of opportunities to drive change, make waves, and leave things a little better than you found them.

As we scout out these potential missions, remember that finding the perfect volunteer match isn't about checking boxes or filling slots—it's about connecting with a cause that resonates with your heart and aligns with your personal mission. It's about finding a challenge that needs your unique talents and sparks your passion. This isn't a one-size-fits-all deal; it's a tailored fit for your individual strengths and aspirations.

Ready to explore? Let's discover where your skills and passions can light up the world.

Decoding Your Skills

The Self-Reflection Toolkit

Before diving into the smorgasbord of causes, let's pause for a skill assessment. Like any good change agent, knowing your own strengths, weaknesses, and interests helps you pick the right assignments and ensures you're equipped for success. Think of this self-reflection as crafting your own undercover identity. One that perfectly aligns with the missions you'll choose to accept.

Here are ten crucial questions to decode your change agent personality profile:

1. What activities energize me and keep me engaged? Why?

2. In group missions, what role do I usually take on?

3. What are the top three skills that allies and mentors compliment me about or say I excel at?

4. What are three challenge areas that test my limits?

5. What activities make time fly for me?

6. Am I more detail-oriented, or do I excel at seeing the big picture? What's an example of this?

7. How have my strengths been an asset in past missions?

8. What environments allow me to operate at peak efficiency? Quiet, bustling, solo, or as part of a team?

9. What motivates me to keep going when a mission gets tough?

10. What causes or issues am I passionate about?

Grab a notebook or open a note on your device and jot down your answers. This self-reflection will be your guide to choosing the right volunteer opportunity, highlighting your unique superpowers and potential growth areas. Keep these insights handy as you peruse the list of causes in the next section. This thoughtful approach ensures you connect with a cause that excites you and aligns perfectly with your strengths and interests.

Now that you are armed with this knowledge, let's explore and find where you can make the most significant impact!

Choosing Your Mission: Navigating the Cause Catalog

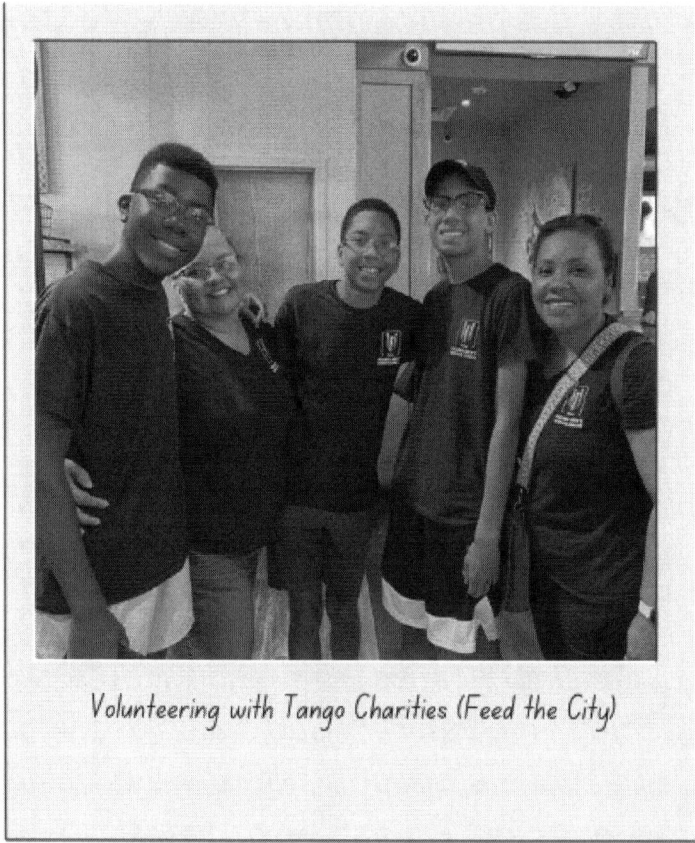

Volunteering with Tango Charities (Feed the City)

Volunteering is like choosing your adventure from a giant empathy buffet. Not every cause will tug at your heartstrings, and that's totally okay. When browsing through the buffet, we just ask that you pick what looks good to you and leave what doesn't. There's no need to complain about the brussels sprouts if you're all about the pizza, right? It's also not cool to make fun of the kid who lives for brussels sprouts or demand that the restaurant remove them from the buffet just because you don't like them. Just focus on what makes you excited to jump in.

So, here are some causes that could take your "just chilling" time to a whole new level of awesome:

- **Accessibility**: Making spaces and experiences open and welcoming to everyone, regardless of their abilities. Imagine a world where everyone gets to play on the same field. You can help make that a reality. Example: Building wheelchair ramps with a non-profit like Texas Ramp Project.

- **Animal Welfare**: From endangered species to neglected and abused animals, aging pets, and those without a home, your voice and actions can be a game-changer for creatures who can't stand up for themselves. Example: Volunteer at a no-kill shelter like Operation Kindness, or maybe you would like to travel to Africa to volunteer at the South Africa Wildlife Reserve.

- **Bullying**: Take a stand and create safer, more inclusive spaces where every kid can learn, grow, and thrive without fear.

- **Child Labor**: Advocate for the rights of children everywhere to have a childhood that's about learning and fun, not work.

- **Disaster Relief**: Whether it's a hurricane, flood, fire, or other natural disaster, step up during these times of crisis to help communities recover and rebuild.

- **Education**: Tutor, mentor, or get involved in programs that make learning accessible and enjoyable for everyone. Education is the key to unlocking dreams.

- **Environment and Sustainability**: Whether it's planting trees, cleaning up rivers, or educating others about reducing waste, your efforts can help ensure a greener, more sustainable planet.

- **Foster Care**: Lend your heart and time to support children and teens in the foster care system or aging out of the foster care system, ensuring they feel valued, connected, and have a safety net.

- **Gender Rights and Equality**: Work toward a world where everyone, regardless of gender, has equal opportunities and rights. Your voice matters in the fight for equality.

- **Homelessness**: Lend a hand in shelters, organize drives, or advocate for policies that help those without a home find safety and support.

- **Hunger**: Get involved in food drives, soup kitchens, or initiatives that aim to ensure no one goes to bed hungry.

- **Immigration and Displacement**: Support communities that are navigating the challenges of immigration and displacement, offering a welcoming hand and necessary resources.

- **Indigenous Rights**: Stand with Indigenous communities to preserve their cultures, lands, and rights.

- **Literacy**: Share the joy of reading by volunteering with literacy programs that help children and adults alike explore new worlds through books.

- **LGBTQ+ Rights and Equality**: Be an ally in creating inclusive spaces where everyone feels safe to be who they are, promoting equality and understanding.

- **Mental Health**: Advocate for mental health awareness, offer your ears to listen, or support initiatives that make mental healthcare accessible to all.

- **Physical Health**: Get involved in programs that promote physical wellness, from sports to nutrition education, making health a priority for communities.

- **Racial Justice and Equity**: Join the movement toward a more just society in which racial background is not a barrier to opportunity, respect, and justice.

- **Veterans**: Give back to those who've served by volunteering with organizations that support veterans and their families.

- **Voting**: Empower your community by encouraging voter registration and participation, ensuring everyone's voice is heard.

- **Water**: Support efforts to ensure everyone has access to clean, safe water—a fundamental human right.

Whew! That's a big list, right? But it's also a treasure trove of opportunity. Each one of these causes can use someone just like you: passionate, ready to make a difference, and maybe even a little bit of a superhero in disguise. Pick a cause (or two or more) that grabs your heart, and then read on.

In the next chapter, we'll equip you with the digital tools the savvy change agent needs to locate and lock in on the ideal volunteer spots. We'll explore how to navigate the internet's vast resources to ensure you're not only finding a great opportunity but also the right fit for your newfound passion. Let's get scouting!

Chapter 7

"I," Internet:

BECOME A CYBER SCOUT AND TRACK DOWN THE PERFECT OPPORTUNITY

So, you've got your heart set on a great cause. Nice! Now, let's explore the "I" of the G.I.V.E. framework—Internet. We understand that not everyone is part of organizations like YMSL or NCL, and not every school hosts volunteer fairs for their students. But the internet is available to most people and can make your search easy.

The internet is your ultimate tool for uncovering golden opportunities to make a difference. It's like your personal radar for scanning the vast expanse of the World Wide Web to pinpoint exactly where your talents and passions can be put to good use and serve the causes you care about.

In this chapter, you'll learn how to harness the power of search engines, navigate the social media landscape, and tap into specialized volunteering databases. It's not just about finding any opportunity to volunteer. It's about finding the right ones that align perfectly with your interests and the causes you care about.

Remember, the best gigs are the ones that get you fired up or touch your heart. When you're passionate about the cause, volunteering doesn't feel like work; it feels like you're part of something bigger.

So, let's get you set up to make a difference.

Volunteer Platforms

Now that you've zeroed in on a cause that stirs your passion, it's time to connect the dots and find the organizations where you can make a real impact. Many volunteer platforms out there can be your launching pad, hooking you up with opportunities that not only do a world of good but also allow you to grow and learn along the way. Whether you're interested in local community service or tackling global challenges, these platforms have a spot just waiting for you.

So, how should you start your search on these platforms? Begin by specifically researching your chosen cause. Most volunteer platforms categorize opportunities by themes—such as environment, education, health, animal welfare, and more—making navigating and finding a match that resonates with your interests easier. This focused approach helps ensure that you're committing to a cause that matters to you and joining an organization whose goals align with your values and aspirations.

Here's why starting with volunteer platforms can be a smart move:

- **Segmented Searches**: These platforms often segment volunteer opportunities by category. This makes it simple to narrow down choices and find projects that align perfectly with your chosen cause.

- **Vetted Opportunities**: Many reputable platforms vet the organizations they list, which means you can feel confident about the authenticity and impact of the volunteer work you choose.

- **Diverse Options**: From short-term assignments to long-term engagements, from on-site work to virtual volunteering, these platforms offer a variety of formats to suit different schedules, skills, and levels of commitment.

- **Resources and Support**: Many platforms provide resources for volunteers beyond listings, such as training materials, advice on how to get the most out of your volunteering experience, and even forums where you can connect with other volunteers.

Here are a few platforms to explore that can transform your free time into something truly impactful:

Doing Good Together

Website: https://www.doinggoodtogether.org

If your family lives near Twin Cities (Minnesota), Miami (Florida), Oakland/East Bay, Silicon Valley, or San Diego (California), Seattle (Washington), Boston (Massachusetts), Baltimore (Maryland), New York City (New York), or St. Louis (Missouri), this website shares family-friendly volunteer opportunities monthly.

DoSomething (Good)

Website: https://www.dosomething.org/us

DoSomething kicked off in '93 with this excellent motto: volunteering can be just as cool as sports. Fast-forward to today, and they're one of the biggest non-profits out there for young folks looking to shake things up and make a difference. Since being founded, they've gotten more than eight million young people hyped about joining in on all sorts of campaigns and programs. And get this, they have members in every single U.S. area code and in 189 countries around the globe. Pretty wild, right? You can be next!

JustServe

Website: https://www.justserve.org

JustServe is your go-to platform for connecting volunteers with community needs, completely free of charge. They're all about inclusion and welcome everyone regardless of race, religion, gender, ethnicity, or sexual orientation to post projects and volunteer. Their tagline: A shared commitment to making a difference. Join us, and let's serve together.

United Way Day of Action

Website: https://www.unitedway.org/get-involved/volunteer

Every year, as June 21 rolls around, tens of thousands of volunteers from hundreds of communities across the globe join forces for United Way's Day of Action. This is more than just a volunteering day; it's a worldwide movement where every little effort leads to massive change. Maybe it's packing backpacks with books to spark a love for reading and boost literacy skills, or perhaps it's getting your hands dirty in community gardens to beautify the neighborhood and promote access to healthy foods. For United Way, the Day of Action reflects their year-round mission: to knit together strong, fair communities where every single person has the chance to flourish.

VolunteerMatch

Website: https://www.volunteermatch.org

The VolunteerMatch platform has matched millions of eager volunteers to various events and activities for tax-exempt organizations, non-profits, non-governmental organizations, and governmental entities needing help. This website makes finding projects that complement your skills and interests easy. Whether you're a newbie or a seasoned pro looking to expand your impact, this platform offers a seamless way to connect with causes that matter.

Volunteer World

Website: https://www.volunteerworld.com/en

But what if you want to volunteer abroad? Volunteer World is the website for you. This volunteer platform helps volunteers find opportunities around the world. Whether you dream of teaching English in a remote village, working with endangered wildlife in conservation projects, or contributing to public health by building wells, Volunteer World offers a gateway to international adventures.

Go Straight to the Source

Using the internet to connect directly with organizations can also be incredibly effective. If you're keen on diving deeper and really engaging with specific groups, here's how you can use direct searches and website visits to your advantage:

1. **Initiate Targeted Searches**: Start with focused internet searches to find non-profits specializing in your chosen cause. Use search terms like "environmental advocacy groups near me," "animal rescue organizations in [your city]," "literacy programs for teens," or "homeless shelters looking for volunteers." Targeted searches like these will lead you to specific organizations in your areas of interest.

2. **Visit Official Websites**: Once you find a potential organization, visit their official website. Most non-profits provide detailed information about their mission, the impact of their work, and specific volunteer opportunities available. Look for sections titled "Get Involved," "How to Help," or "Volunteer With Us" to understand what types of volunteer roles are available.

3. **Check for Teen-Specific Programs**: Many organizations have programs specifically designed for high school students or young volunteers. These programs are tailored to provide a meaningful experience that is also manageable alongside school commitments.

4. **Review Social Media Pages**: Don't overlook an organization's social media pages. These can be great sources of up-to-date information on current initiatives, upcoming events, and calls for volunteers. Following these pages can also give you insights into the organization's community engagement and active projects.

5. **Connect via Community Boards and Forums**: Places like Nextdoor, community Face-

book groups, or even local forums often have posts about volunteer opportunities. These platforms can provide insights into how active the organization is locally and what kind of help they're currently seeking.

6. **Reach Out Proactively**: If you find an organization that resonates with your goals but doesn't have clear volunteer sign-up information, don't hesitate to contact them directly. Sending an email or direct message through social media can be very effective. Be sure to:

   ○ Introduce yourself: Briefly explain who you are and why you are interested in their work.

   ○ Express your interest: Clearly state that you are looking for volunteer opportunities and ask if there are any positions available.

   ○ Mention your skills: If you have specific skills that could benefit their programs, mention these. It can make you a more attractive candidate for volunteer roles.

7. **Be Prepared to Follow Up**: If you don't get

a response immediately, it's appropriate to send a polite follow-up a week or two later. Sometimes, messages can get overlooked in busy periods.

By following these steps, you will find volunteer opportunities that match your interests and abilities, and demonstrate initiative and commitment—qualities that organizations highly value. So, start your search and make those connections.

Don't Sleep on Local Government Opportunities

Opportunities to volunteer for your city are also just one Google search away. Many cities have offices that recruit volunteers. For example, Plano, Texas, has a centralized volunteer office called the VIP program. This office recruits thousands of adults, teens, college students, and groups. Volunteers get placed in the city's libraries, animal services, parks and recreation, unpaid internships, special projects and events, and more.

Try a Google search with your city's name plus "city council volunteer opportunities," "student volunteer opportunities," "library volunteers," or the name of another city department that interests you.

Virtual Volunteering

There are a lot of reasons why in-person volunteering may not work for you. Your parents may work, so transportation to and from a non-profit during the workday isn't possible. You might have a health condition that makes it unsafe to be around large groups of people. You may experience social anxiety when you're around a bunch of strangers. Maybe you live in a small town, and there are just not a lot of places to volunteer. Don't worry. That's where virtual volunteering comes in.

Volunteering virtually allows you to contribute to worthy causes that fit into your schedule. This makes it easier to juggle school, hobbies, and volunteering. Plus, you gain experience all while wearing your favorite pajamas.

Here are some examples of how some non-profits use virtual volunteers:

Be My Eyes

Website: https://support.bemyeyes.com/hc/en-us/categories/360000920938-Sighted-Volunteer

Be My Eyes is a revolutionary app that connects sighted volunteers like you to visually impaired people around the globe who need help with daily tasks. By "a little help," we mean anything from checking expiration dates on food to reading instructions or picking out a cool outfit.

Imagine being someone's eyes through your phone's camera, helping them navigate challenges you might take for granted. It's not just about the assistance but the connection, the stories you'll hear, and the people you'll meet. You'll be part of a massive, caring community that's all about making the world more accessible, one pair of eyes at a time.

Volunteering with Be My Eyes is super flexible. You can jump in whenever you're free, between homework, after practice, or while chilling at home. You'll get calls through the app, and if you're busy, no stress—the call can be passed on to another volunteer.

So, why not add "Digital Hero" to your resume? By joining Be My Eyes, you're not just killing time; you're making a real, tangible difference in someone's life, and all it takes is the tap of a button. Let's use technology to bring us closer, to bridge gaps, and to create a community that truly looks out for each other. Ready to be someone's eyes?

Best Buddies International

Website: https://www.bestbuddies.org/what-we-do/ebuddies/

Imagine being part of a global movement that's all about making genuine connections and ensuring everyone has a friend, especially those who might feel left out or sidelined because they live with intellectual or developmental disabilities. That's where Best Buddies enters the spotlight, inviting you to be a game-changer from your screen.

Best Buddies is an incredible global non-profit that's tearing down the barriers of social isolation and building a world of inclusion and friendship. How cool is that? And with their eBuddies program, you can make a real impact, no matter where you are.

Here's the scoop: By volunteering with eBuddies, you're signing up to be a part of someone's life in a meaningful way. You'll exchange messages, share stories, and be that go-to person for someone who might not have many friends. It's about more than just texts and emails; it's about creating bonds that defy distances and differences.

Distributed Proofreaders Foundation

Website: https://www.pgdp.net/c/

All right, picture this: In the world of *Fahrenheit 451*, books are public enemy number one, destined to be torched by firemen. But what if I told you there's a rebellion brewing, one that you can join without ever leaving your room? Enter the Distributed Proofreaders Foundation, the digital underground fighting to save public domain books from oblivion. Never heard of public domain books before? Public domain books are books that are no longer under copyright protection and are freely accessible to the public. These books can be used without seeking permission or paying the original author.

Imagine donning your virtual cape and joining a squad of literary rebels, each one dedicated to outsmarting the dystopian doom of disappearing texts. This isn't just editing—it's an act of defiance. By hunting down typos, polishing sentences, and re-viving the classics, you're not just correcting texts; you're snatching them from the flames, ensuring they're immortalized online for all to read, free of charge.

Every page you turn, every error you catch, is a strike against the world of *Fahrenheit 451*. You're not just volunteering but preserving culture, knowl-edge, and freedom, one word at a time. And in doing so, you're sharpening your skills, joining a global network of fellow word warriors, and making your mark on the literary world.

So, are you ready to stand up to the firemen, to be the hero books need? The Distributed Proofreaders Foundation is your battleground, and the fight to save literature from the flames starts with you. Join the cause, and let's turn the tide against censor-ship, one typo at a time.

Girls Inc.

Website: https://www.girlsinc.org/get-involved/become-a-social-media-ambassador

If you're scrolling through your feed looking for something impactful to do with your social media savvy, here's your chance to be part of something bigger. Have you ever heard of Girls Inc.? This incredible non-profit inspires and empowers girls to be strong, smart, and bold. Through mentorship, education, and advocacy, Girls Inc. helps girls navigate the challenges of growing up and break through gender, economic, and social barriers.

Now, here's where you come in. Girls Inc. is looking for Social Media Ambassadors—yes, that means you! Use your Instagram, TikTok, X (formerly Twitter), or whatever platform you love to shout out about a wonderful cause. Imagine the likes, shares, and impact you could generate by crafting engaging posts, stories, and videos that empower girls.

Volunteering as a Social Media Ambassador is more than just a chance to beef up your resume (though it definitely will); it's about being part of a global movement, connecting with like-minded peers, and making a tangible difference in the lives of young girls who can benefit from having strong role models like you.

Whether you're a wizard with hashtags, a master of the perfect TikTok dance challenge, or just someone who genuinely wants to make a difference while honing your digital skills, Girls Inc. offers you the platform to be that change. So, what do you say?

Ready to turn your social media prowess into a superpower for good? Let's do this and show the world the power of volunteers supporting girls!

Humane Society of the United States

Website: https://www.humanesociety.org/volunteer

Looking for a way to make a difference, take action, and possibly rack up some good vibes (and maybe even volunteer hours) from your own home? Let's talk about The Humane Society of the United States (HSUS)—a powerhouse fighting to give animals a better tomorrow.

The HSUS isn't just about rescuing puppies and kittens (though, let's be honest, that's a pretty awesome part of it). They're on the front lines battling animal cruelty on a massive scale—think major operations like puppy mills, wildlife abuse, and inhumane farming practices. They're all about ensuring every furry, feathery, or scaly friend gets a shot at the life they deserve.

You might think, *Sounds great, but I'm crazy busy with school, sports, and life.* No sweat! The HSUS has tailored its volunteering opportunities to fit your digital, on-the-go lifestyle. By volunteering virtually, you can lend your voice, social media savvy, or organizational skills to campaigns that need exactly what you have to offer.

There are multiple at-home options at HSUS. For example, the Animal Protection Organization Research Volunteers help build and maintain a list of organizations in the animal protection space.

This initiative plays a big part in expanding HSUS outreach. Volunteers conduct online research to fill any knowledge gaps in the animal protection field, including how HSUS's network of organizations connects with animal shelters, rescue operations, law enforcement, and spay/neuter initiatives. These findings are then collected and entered into an online form. This effort enhances their database and strengthens their collective impact across communities involved in animal welfare.

Mozilla

Website: https://www.mozilla.org/en-US/contribute/

This non-profit is for tech enthusiasts. There are tons of virtual opportunities where your coding skills, creative genius, and passion for an open internet can truly make a difference. Mozilla is the powerhouse behind the Firefox browser. It isn't just an ordinary tech company; it's a non-profit that's all about keeping the web open and accessible for everyone. Think of it as the guardian of the internet universe, battling against the forces that threaten our online freedom and privacy. And the best part? You can join the ranks as a virtual volunteer!

As a tech-savvy volunteer, you'll dive into projects that could range from squashing bugs in open-source software to designing wicked web pages that champion internet literacy. Imagine contributing to real-world projects like Firefox, which millions use to explore the digital world safely and freely. Or perhaps you'll lend your skills to developing new tech that protects users' privacy from the ever-watchful eyes of Big Data.

But it's not all about coding; Mozilla believes in empowering internet users everywhere to understand, shape, and defend the web. You could help educate your peers about digital rights, create content that demystifies the complex world of internet health, or even advocate for policies that ensure the web remains a global public resource.

Volunteering with Mozilla is a killer way to network with tech professionals and get a real taste of working in the field—all from your own home.

Ready to be part of something huge? To not just dream about a better internet but to actively build it? Mozilla's waiting for you. Let's code, create, and change the world together. Your mission, should you choose to accept it, starts now.

National Archives

Website: https://www.archives.gov/citizen-archivist

Have you ever wondered where all the cool, secret stuff from our country's history is kept? Like, the original Declaration of Independence, or those top-secret letters between historical figures? That's where the National Archives steps in. It's basically the treasure chest of American history. But here's the twist: They're not just about keeping old documents safe; they're on a mission to make history accessible and engaging for everyone, including you.

Now, imagine being a part of that mission without even having to leave your room. Through virtual volunteering with the National Archives, you can dive into the world of historical documents, photographs, and records, helping to bring the past to life for people all over the world. You could be transcribing handwritten letters from the 1800s, tagging photos from historical events to make them easier to find, or even creating digital exhibits that highlight cool moments in history.

Why should you care? Well, apart from the bragging rights of being a history detective, you're also getting a backstage pass to the stories that shaped our nation. It's a killer way to show off your skills in research, technology, and attention to detail.

So, if you're into history, tech, or just looking for a unique way to make a difference, the National Archives' virtual volunteering program could be your next big adventure. Get ready to explore the hidden corners of America's past, uncover secrets, and share them with the world. Let's make history, not just learn it.

Operation Gratitude

Website: https://www.operationgratitude.com/volunteer/anywhere/letters/

This organization is all about sending a mega dose of appreciation and support to those who serve our country—think people in the military, first responders, and veterans. It's like a giant, countrywide thank-you note, and you get to be a part of it.

By volunteering for Operation Gratitude's letter-writing campaign, you're not just filling up a page; you're filling someone's day with joy, respect, and a reminder that what they do matters. Picture this: Someone far from home, maybe feeling homesick or stressed, opens a letter from you, a total stranger, just to say "thanks" and "we're thinking of you." That can turn a rough day into a great one. And the cool part? You can do it from anywhere—your bedroom, the coffee shop, or between binge-watching episodes of your favorite series.

It's a simple act, but it packs a punch. Plus, it's a killer way to boost your writing skills, rack up some volunteer hours, and make a tangible impact on someone's life. Operation Gratitude is about bridging gaps and building connections, one letter at a time. So grab some friends, get creative, and join a movement that's all about gratitude and respect.

The Trevor Project

Website: https://www.thetrevorproject.org/volunteer/

The Trevor Project is a safe space for LGBTQ+ teens who need a friend who is ready to listen, understand, and support them 24/7 with no judgment, just love. Whether they're seeking a listening ear during tough times, searching for resources to understand their identity better, or simply looking for a space where they feel accepted, The Trevor Project is there. It's more than just crisis intervention; it's about building a community where young people can feel accepted.

You must be eighteen years or older and willing to provide empathy and understanding to volunteer with The Trevor Project. It's an opportunity to touch lives, offer hope, and advocate for a future where these kids feel accepted. Your actions can turn the tide for someone who feels alone, reinforcing that they matter, their feelings are valid, and they're never alone. It's about creating a world of kindness and acceptance where every teen can look forward to a brighter, more inclusive tomorrow.

The Smithsonian

Website: https://www.si.edu/volunteer/DigitalVolunteers

The Smithsonian isn't just a collection of awesome museums. It's a world where history, art, science, and culture collide. It's a global leader in preserving what makes us tick, from the dinosaurs to space explorations, and everything in between. And guess what? You can be a part of this epic adventure, all from your laptop!

Volunteering with the Smithsonian virtually is like getting an all-access pass to the coolest behind-the-scenes action. You could be transcribing historical documents, bringing ancient texts to life for everyone to explore online. Or maybe you're into the arts? Help curate digital exhibitions that people around the world can visit from their couches. Science buffs can get in on the action, too, assisting in research projects that span from the ocean's depths to the universe's edges.

It's your chance to connect with like-minded folks who believe in making information accessible everywhere. You'll gain insane skills, meet experts in areas you're curious about, and contribute to projects that matter.

Ready to make a real impact, expand your horizons, and be part of a community that's shaping the future of knowledge? The Smithsonian's virtual volunteering opportunities are calling your name. Let's make history together.

Vetting the Non-Profit

Keep in mind as you research, not everyone that calls themselves a charity is legit. Some non-profits are scams that spend pennies of every dollar they raise on the causes they claim to help. The rest of the money goes to lining the pockets of the founders and staff. Not cool.

Before you give your time or money to a charity fraud, do your homework and investigate the organization to make sure they will spend donors' hard-earned money responsibly or that you're associating yourself with an organization worthy of your time.

How do you do that? Websites like CharityNavigator.org and CharityWatch.org rate thousands of non-profits and put the frauds out there on blast. The bottom line is you need to be careful.

And there you have it, change agent. In this chapter, you've mastered the art of using the internet to track down great causes and charities that serve them, while also verifying they're legit. You don't have to leave your bedroom to make a difference because virtual volunteering can be done wherever your mission calls you. Technology is the real MVP here, serving as your high-tech gadget that connects you to meaningful operations and allows you to contribute effectively from your secret base.

In the next chapter, it's time to take the leap and volunteer, the "V" in the G.I.V.E. framework. Get ready to deploy into the field, agent, translating your digital reconnaissance into real-world actions that showcase your capabilities and compassion.

Chapter 8

"V," Volunteer:

TAKE YOUR ACTION STATIONS AND MAKE YOUR MARK

Before you get to the heart of the mission (volunteering), let's quickly recap your journey with the G .I.V.E. framework. You started with "G" to lock down a Great Cause. You found a cause that sparks a fire in your heart, like saving the planet, championing animal rights, or coding the next big app for social good.

Then, with "I" for the Internet, you turned to our trusty digital wingman to sleuth out the perfect opportunities. Harnessing the power of the internet, you researched, connected, and planned your approach. Now, armed with passion and insights, you're ready to make light work of the "V" for Volunteering. It's time to leap into action, make a real difference, and bring your Summer of Service to life!

Setting Realistic Goals

It's go-time at the "Action Stations"! As you gear up to dive into your heroic deeds, let's take a moment to strategize and set the stage like the savvy operatives you are. Setting realistic goals is akin to equipping yourself with the right gadgets for a secret mission. Just as you wouldn't pack a snorkel for a desert operation, it's essential to align your goals with the mission at hand.

First up, scope out the landscape. What's your summer looking like? Are you free as a bird or juggling ninja training with a part-time gig at the secret lair (also known as the local coffee shop)? Be honest about the time you can commit. Volunteering isn't about stretching yourself thinner than Spider-Man's web; it's about making impactful contributions without turning into a sleep-deprived zombie.

Next, tailor your mission to fit your skills and interests (the information from the previous chapter will come in handy here). This will help make sure that you are not just effective but also genuinely engaged in what you are doing.

Are you passionate about digital art? Consider offering your skills to design a website for a local charity, helping them amplify their online presence and reach.

Are you the next Messi at soccer? You could channel that talent into coaching a youth team or volunteering at a soccer camp for underprivileged kids.

This step is akin to choosing your superhero costume. Sure, all capes are cool, but you need something that not only looks good but also enhances your ability to act effectively.

Think about the skills you can bring to the table and match them with needs in the community.

If you excel in writing, look into helping with writing social media content or creating engaging content for non-profit newsletters.

If you're a tech whiz, offer to manage or improve the IT infrastructure for a local non-profit.

This approach allows you to make the most impact, turning your volunteering time into a supercharged effort that benefits both you and your chosen cause. This customization is key—it ensures you're not only comfortable and confident in your volunteer role but also incredibly impactful, moving smoothly and striking powerfully where it counts.

Remember, change agent, the goal here isn't just to fill your summer with activities but to choose missions that light you up and make a tangible difference. Set your sights on achievable targets—think more "saving the neighborhood park" and less "solving world peace by August."

And finally, jot down your goals. Whether it's in a top-secret notebook or your trusty smartphone, keeping a record will help you stay on track. Plus, ticking off completed missions? Super satisfying. Here's an example of what that might look like:

This Week:

- Identify potential charities by Tuesday.

- Draft inquiry emails on Wednesday.

- Send emails by Friday.

- Set up a follow-up reminder for next Wednesday.

This Month:

- Attend a volunteer orientation session.

- Start volunteering at chosen organization.

- Write a reflection on the initial experience.

Ongoing:

- Weekly check-in with volunteer coordinator.

- Monthly goal review and adjustment.

Using this structured approach not only keeps your volunteer missions organized but also enhances your motivation by visually tracking your accomplishments.

So, let's get those goals in gear, change agent. With a clear plan, you're not just flying blind into the night but soaring toward success. Onward to making your mark and transforming this summer into a saga of service!

When You Commit, Show Up!

Now that we've charted the course accurately, it's time to discuss the heart of every mission—showing up and putting your plan into action. Not just physically being there, but being all in. Think of it like a superhero swooping in to save the day; they don't just make a brief appearance, wave hello, and disappear. They're there for the entire battle, from the dramatic entrance to the final showdown.

Commitment is your secret weapon. It's what elevates you from a casual volunteer to a change-making powerhouse. When you commit to a volunteering gig, you're not just filling a spot; you're making a promise to the organization and to yourself. You're declaring, "I'm here to make a difference, and I won't step back until our goals are achieved."

But how do you ensure you're truly putting this commitment into action? It starts with preparation and presence. Prepare for each volunteering session as if it were a crucial mission. Know what's expected, bring the necessary tools, and arrive ready to engage fully. Each time you follow through with your commitment, you build trust and reliability—not just among the people you're helping but also in the eyes of potential future allies, mentors, and even colleges or employers. Think of it as collecting hero points; the more you accumulate, the stronger and more extensive your network of alliances becomes.

Fully committing also means diving deep into your mission, immersing yourself in experiences that challenge you, teach you, and ultimately, transform you into a more formidable version of yourself. It's about making a profound impact, not just skimming through the experience.

So, as you embark on this volunteering journey, remember: When you commit, show up like the hero you are destined to be. Give it your all, stick to your plan, and watch as your actions create waves of positive change. The world doesn't just need more bystanders; it needs heroes who are ready to step up and make a real difference. Let's be those heroes.

Next, we'll show you how to get the most out of your volunteering mission. Read on to learn how to enjoy yourself, engage with others and your cause, and expand your experience.

Chapter 9

"E," Elevate Your Mission Experience:

ENJOY, ENGAGE, AND EXPAND

This chapter reveals the hidden perks of volunteering—the amazing benefits that go way beyond just helping out. In the world of secret missions and making a difference, volunteering isn't just about giving; it's about what you get back too. Here, you'll learn how to make the most out of every part of your volunteering adventures.

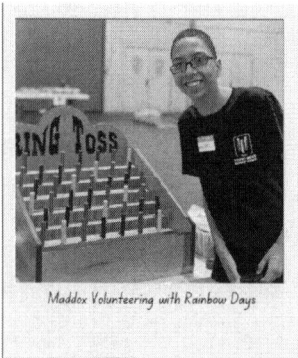

Maddox Volunteering with Rainbow Days

We'll dive into three big ideas: enjoying what you do, really getting involved in your tasks and with the people you meet, and growing from your experiences. Each part is super important, not just to make your volunteering successful but to help you grow as a person. You'll find that volunteering can introduce you to new friends, teach you new things, and help you discover more about who you are.

As we go through this chapter, you'll find tips and tricks to help you dive deeper into your volunteer work, enjoy the good feelings that come from helping others, and use what you learn to see the world differently.

Get ready to do good things and elevate how you see yourself and your world. Let's start this journey together, making sure every moment you spend volunteering is as fun and rewarding for you as it is helpful for others.

So, listen up! It's time to transform your volunteering into exciting missions that not only change the world but also help you grow.

Enjoy the Thrill of the Chase

First off, let's talk about the adrenaline rush. Volunteering isn't just about giving back; it's about having an experience that rivals the excitement of any spy mission. Did you feel the buzz when you cracked the code of someone's smile as you helped them out? That's the universe high-fiving you, change agent.

Like any seasoned spy who craves the rush of a successfully completed mission, take a moment to revel in the joy your actions brought not just to others but to yourself. Laughter shared while painting a mural or the warmth from a grateful nod across a soup kitchen—these are your mission mementos.

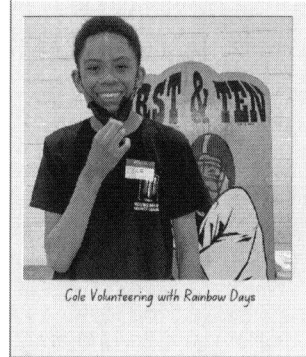

Cole Volunteering with Rainbow Days

This thrill is what keeps you coming back for more. Each task you undertake, whether it's organizing books at a library or leading a group in a community clean-up, injects a sense of adventure into your day. You never know what challenges you'll face or what victories you'll secure. Each interaction, every grateful smile, and every problem solved adds to your repertoire of experiences, enhancing your skills and deepening your understanding of the world.

Moreover, the exhilaration doesn't end when the day is done. The stories you collect, the teamwork you experience, and the gratitude you receive fuel your enthusiasm for future missions.

They remind you why you stepped into the world of volunteering: to make a difference and feel the immense satisfaction that comes from knowing you've left a positive mark on the world. Each mission, no matter how small, builds your confidence and affirms your ability to influence change.

So, embrace the thrill of the chase. Let it motivate you to push boundaries, explore new territories of service, and continue to grow as a change agent. Remember, every mission counts, and every effort you make adds to the collective good. You are not just passing time; you are making history.

Engage in Empathy

Every person you meet on your mission carries a backstory as intricate and layered as any top-secret dossier. By stepping into their shoes, you've practiced empathy, which might just be a change agent's most powerful yet underrated gadget.

Empathy is the ability to understand and share another person's feelings. It's not feeling sorry for someone you see hurting or struggling. It's about seeing the world through someone else's eyes and feeling what they feel, which is crucial for anyone on a mission to make a difference.

This skill allows you to decode the secret signals and hidden messages that people convey, not with their words but through their emotions and reactions. It's what helps you build deep, genuine connections that can bridge worlds and break down barriers.

There is a difference between feeling sorry for someone and having empathy for them. Understanding the difference between sympathy and empathy is crucial if you want to take meaningful action to help someone.

Feeling Sorry for Someone Who is Homeless:

When you feel sorry for someone who is homeless, you might see them on the street and think, *That's so sad,* or *I wish things were different for them.*

This reaction is often fleeting—a moment of pity or sorrow that acknowledges the person's situation but doesn't engage deeply with their feelings or experiences. You may feel bad about their situation, but this feeling doesn't necessarily drive you to understand more deeply or act to help. You also may think to yourself, *Why don't they just get a job?*

Having Empathy for Someone Who is Homeless:

Empathy involves putting yourself in the shoes of the person who is homeless, trying to understand what daily life is like for them. It's asking yourself, *What challenges do they face every day? How do they feel being in this situation?*

Empathy drives a deeper connection and often compels you to help or support in a more informed, considerate way. For example, instead of just feeling bad, you might strike up a conversation with the person, learn about their specific needs, and provide direct help—like a meal, warm clothing, or information about local resources—or even advocate for systemic changes that address the root causes of homelessness.

Your interaction will change your perspective. For example, we've interacted with many people who do have jobs but are still homeless.

As you reflect on your interactions, think about how they have shifted your perspective, almost like adjusting the lens on your spyglass. How have these moments changed the way you view challenges, solutions, and the impact of your actions?

Understanding others' feelings and viewpoints can transform the way you approach future missions, making you not only a better volunteer but a more compassionate human being.

Consider the profound impact of empathy on your missions: It enhances your ability to serve effectively and sensitively, ensuring that your help is not just needed but also appropriate and kind. It's this understanding that can turn a good volunteer into a great one, changing simple acts of service into powerful acts of kindness that resonate deeply with everyone involved.

So, as you continue your journey, keep honing this invaluable skill. Engage deeply, listen intently, and let empathy guide your actions. By doing so, you're not just completing missions—you're changing lives, including your own.

Expand Your Arsenal

Lastly, as a volunteer, each task you tackle upgrades a whole suite of skills that are now at your disposal for future missions. Teamwork, leadership, and problem-solving under pressure—these aren't just lines on your resume; they're badges of honor, evidence of your readiness to take on whatever the world throws your way. But the benefits don't stop there.

You also gain invaluable skills in communication, as you learn to interact with diverse groups of people. Adaptability becomes second nature as you navigate various environments and challenges. Organizational skills are sharpened as you manage tasks and coordinate with others to meet goals on time. Furthermore, creativity is often called into play, requiring you to think outside the box and innovate solutions to unexpected problems.

Each of these skills enriches your personal and professional life, preparing you not only for future volunteer opportunities but also for any career or community role you might pursue. They demonstrate your ability to handle complex situations, work collaboratively, and lead with compassion and insight—qualities that are highly valued in every field.

As you reflect on these newfound abilities, consider how they enrich your resume. For a young adult stepping into the future, these experiences not only show commitment and capability on paper but also set you apart in college applications and job interviews. Each skill boosts your profile and prepares you for your next covert operation, be it in college, your career, or your next volunteer venture. Every challenge you meet, and every skill you develop is another star on your resume, highlighting your proactive spirit and versatility in facing diverse challenges.

Each volunteer opportunity is a chance to fill in gaps on your resume. We thought it would be helpful to see how volunteer work can beef up a resume. On the next page, you'll see an example of a resume for someone who was strategic in how she demonstrated her interest in the technology field.

SAMANTHA LEWIS

(555) 987-6543 | samantha.lee@example.com
LinkedIn: linkedin.com/in/samantha-lee-tech

Award-winning high school technologist with a 3.9 GPA, experienced in IT support and web development for community organizations. Proficient in Python, HTML, CSS, and JavaScript, I bring a track record of improving digital literacy and enhancing website user engagement. Committed to applying problem-solving skills and technical expertise in an entry-level IT role.

EDUCATION

Tech City High School, Tech City, State
GPA: 3.9/4.0 (unweighted)
Expected Graduation: June 2025

ONLINE COURSES AND CERTIFICATIONS

- Python for Everybody (Coursera)
- Introduction to Computer Science and Programming Using Python (edX)

VOLUNTEER EXPERIENCE

TECH TUTOR

Community Tech Hub, Tech City, State
January 2023–Present

- Teach basic computer skills, internet safety, and introductory programming to community members of all ages, enhancing digital literacy in the community.
- Develop and deliver weekly workshops on using software applications effectively, including word processors, spreadsheets, and presentation tools.
- Assist in setting up and maintaining computer hardware and software, gaining practical IT support experience.

WEB DEVELOPER VOLUNTEER

Non-Profit Organization, Tech City, State
May 2022–December 2022

- Volunteered to build and update websites for local non-profit organizations using HTML, CSS, and JavaScript.
- Improved user interface designs for three non-profit websites, increasing user engagement by 30 percent.
- Collaborated with non-profit staff to understand and translate their needs into effective web solutions.

IT SUPPORT VOLUNTEER
Tech City Annual Science Fair, Tech City, State
April 2022

- Provided IT support during the Tech City Annual Science Fair, troubleshooting software and hardware issues for exhibitors.
- Set up and managed network connections for over fifty participants, ensuring the event's smooth operation.
- Gained valuable experience in fast-paced problem-solving and technical communication.

SKILLS

- **Programming Languages**: Proficient in Python, HTML, CSS, and JavaScript.
- **Technical Support**: Experienced in troubleshooting hardware, software, and network issues.
- **Communication**: Strong ability to explain complex technical concepts to non-technical audiences.
- **Teamwork**: Demonstrated success in working collaboratively on technology projects.
- **Adaptability**: Quickly learns new technologies and adapts to changing technical environments.

AWARDS AND RECOGNITIONS

- Tech Innovator Award
- Community Tech Hub, 2023
- Outstanding Volunteer, Non-Profit Organization Web Development, 2022

PROJECTS

- **Community Website Redesign for the XYZ Non-Profit**: Redesigned the website to improve navigation and aesthetic appeal and implemented a responsive design for mobile compatibility.
- **Python Project for Library Management System**: Developed a simple library management system to track books and members, practicing Python programming and database management.

AWARDS AND RECOGNITIONS

- Tech Innovator Award, Community Tech Hub, 2023
- Outstanding Volunteer, XYZ Non-Profit Organization Web Development, 2022

This resume is an example of how a high school student can leverage volunteer experience to boost a tech-focused resume. Samantha used her extensive involvement in various IT and computer education roles to fill gaps and illustrate her deep commitment to both tech and community service.

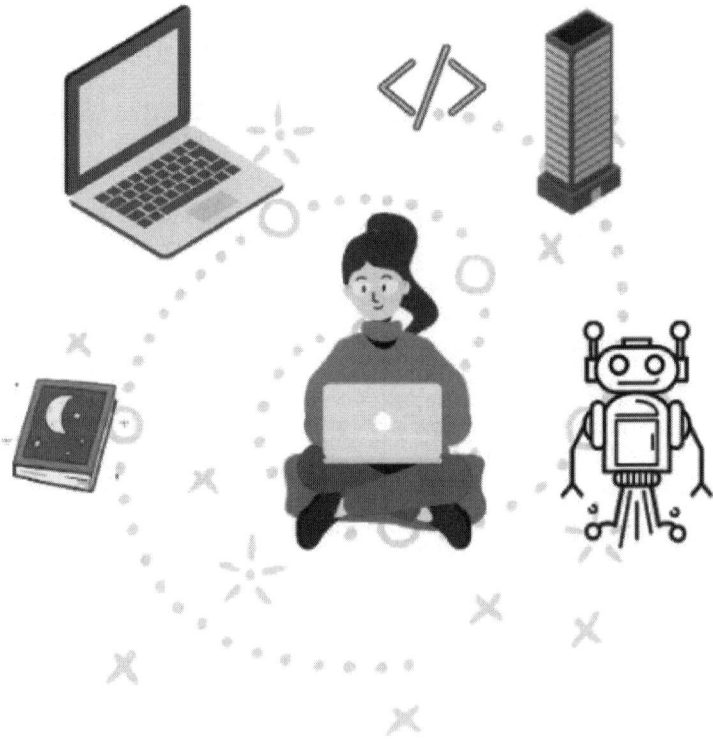

Samantha's volunteer experiences detail her accomplishments that mirror job responsibilities in the tech world. For example, teaching at the Community Tech Hub showcases her ability to educate and enhance digital literacy, crucial for any role requiring technical communication skills. Her experience in developing and leading workshops demonstrates her leadership and ability to convey complex information in an accessible way—key traits for any aspiring IT professional.

Plus, her role as a Web Developer Volunteer goes beyond basic participation by highlighting her direct impact on improving user engagement through interface enhancements. This kind of hands-on experience with real-world applications of HTML, CSS, and JavaScript provides concrete examples of her skills that are highly appealing to potential employers or internship coordinators.

In the IT Support Volunteer role, Samantha showed her technical and problem-solving skills under pressure, a common scenario in many tech jobs. Handling technical issues at a large event like the Tech City Annual Science Fair also indicates her ability to manage stressful situations effectively, ensuring technology supports rather than hinders important events.

Each role on her resume reflects her technical skills as well as her ability to apply these skills in different environments. Her volunteer experiences show potential employers that she has the technical skills they're looking for plus a proven track record of using these skills in a variety of settings.

In summary, Samantha's resume effectively uses her volunteer experiences to provide proof of her skills and impact. This approach transforms her resume from a simple list of tasks into evidence of her career readiness, making her a strong candidate for internships in the industry. Her resume shows how volunteer roles can enhance a resume, especially for high school students looking to get their foot in the door.

As you go on your missions, change agent, remember to enjoy, engage, and expand to heighten your volunteering experience. We're almost through, but the next chapter will discuss the after-action review, an important step of reflection that can impact your future.

Chapter 10

After-Action Review:

LESSONS FROM THE FIELD

Every time you finish a mission, make sure to jot down the key moments in your secret journal (or on your smartphone for the tech-savvy change agents). Write about the highs and the lows, and the surprises along the way. What moments made you super proud? Which challenges really pushed you to your limits? This isn't just about remembering good times; it's crucial intel for your next mission in giving back.

Why is this practice so helpful? First off, writing things down gives you a solid record of what you did and what happened. This is great for looking back over time to see how much you've grown or when you're showing others what you've achieved and learned.

Second, reflecting helps you understand yourself better. It shows you what you're good at and what you might need to work on. When you think about what was tough, you can figure out new ways to handle similar situations in the future. Recognizing your proud moments helps you know what to keep doing or do even more next time.

Plus, reviewing your actions lets you tweak your methods. If you see something that could have gone better, you can change your plan for next time. This keeps you sharp and ready for whatever your next adventure might throw at you.

So, don't skip this step. Taking the time to review your mission makes you a smarter, more prepared agent of change. Each review is a chance to level up your skills and be an even better hero on your next mission.

Here is a format for what your reflections might look like:

1. Highlights and Achievements:

- What worked? Jot down the parts of the volunteering experience that were successful.

- Key accomplishments: List the specific achievements that made you feel proud.

- Example: We volunteered at Rays of Light, providing respite care for kids with special needs. We were matched with a child with Angelman syndrome, and we didn't know anything about this syndrome, so we did a quick search to learn more. Kids with Angelman syndrome usually smile and laugh a lot, and they are very friendly. They might not talk much, and walking can be a bit wobbly. They also find learning new things tougher than other kids. We let our new friend hold our hands to keep his balance and followed as he led us through the building. We had to be patient because he wasn't able to tell us what he wanted to do. We were able to connect with our new friend by treating him kindly and with a lot of patience.

2. **Challenges and Lessons:**

   ○ What was challenging? Identify moments where you faced difficulties.

   ○ Lessons learned: Consider what these challenges taught you about volunteering, teamwork, and your personal strengths and weaknesses.

   ○ Example: There were kids with all kinds of abilities. Some wore helmets, some were in wheelchairs, and some required three to four different buddies to keep them safe. It was really eye-opening to see kids with so many different struggles. Our new friend wasn't interested in, or able to do, many of the activities that Rays of Light planned for the evening, like the balloon artist, movie, and coloring. He also wasn't potty-trained, so we had to make sure he didn't have an accident. After the first hour of walking around nonstop, we needed a break, but our friend wanted to keep moving, so we took turns taking a break while the others kept moving with him.

3. **Emotional Responses:**

- Emotional highs and lows: Recall moments that were particularly moving or frustrating.

- Impact on you: Reflect on how these experiences have affected your view of volunteering and your role in making a difference.

- Example: Even though our new friend was always smiling, we wondered what it was like for him to be unable to ask for what he needed or wanted. We worried that he would have an accident because we didn't see the signs that he needed to go to the bathroom. We realized that we take a lot of things for granted that are actually really hard or impossible for some kids to do.

4. **Future Plans:**

- Improvements for next time: Based on your reflections, think about what you might change in future volunteering efforts.

- New goals: Set specific objectives for your next mission based on what you've learned.

- Example: The next time we work with nonverbal kids, we'll know that we need to introduce activities like the puppet show, dress-up, and games to them. Experimenting with different kinds of activities will make the time more enjoyable for a new friend with disabilities.

5. **Action Steps:**

- Immediate next steps: Outline a few actions you can take right away to continue your journey in service.

- Long-term aspirations: Consider how you can incorporate these lessons into your long-term goals for giving back.

- Example: Working with young kids is a lot of fun but also a lot of responsibility. We'll sign up to volunteer again because the more we go, the more familiar our faces will be to the kids.

Using a structured reflection approach allows you to process your experiences thoroughly and plan more effectively for future volunteering endeavors. It transforms your reflections from mere memories into a strategic plan that enhances your effectiveness and impact as a volunteer. This approach ensures that each mission you undertake not only contributes to your personal growth but also maximizes your contribution to the causes you care about.

What's Next?

So, what does the future hold for you, change agent? Perhaps it's infiltrating new territories of volunteer work, or maybe it's scouting for new recruits and bringing your friends to join you on a mission. Whatever it is, remember that the world needs heroes willing to brave the unknown for the greater good. And you, my friend, have proven yourself one of the best.

As you stand at this juncture, consider the paths unwalked and the adventures that await. Each choice you make now can lead to new challenges and further your journey as a champion for change. Think about the areas you haven't explored yet. Is there a cause that tugs at your heartstrings, or a community you've yet to connect with? Now might be the perfect time to extend your reach.

Alternatively, look back on your recent missions and ask yourself where you can deepen your impact. Could you take on a leadership role in an ongoing project? Or perhaps there's an opportunity to refine the processes of a volunteer program, making it more effective and far-reaching. Reflecting on your past successes and lessons can illuminate how you can enhance these initiatives.

Scouting for new recruits and encouraging your friends to join your volunteer efforts can amplify your impact significantly. Bringing in fresh energy and new perspectives strengthens the overall effort and ensures the sustainability of the good work you've started. By teaching others to navigate the complexities of volunteer service, you foster a new generation of change agents who can carry forward the torch of service and advocacy.

No matter which path you choose, keep in mind that a change agent never sits still. Volunteering is a dynamic adventure that requires continuous learning, adaptation, and passion. Stay curious, stay committed, and stay ready to jump at new opportunities to make a difference.

The future is wide open, filled with potential for more adventures and impact. So gear up, set your sights on the horizons of change, and prepare to push the boundaries of what you can achieve. The world is waiting for your next bold move, change agent. What will it be?

Long-Term Impact

Every superhero saga has its defining moments, and your Summer of Service is poised to be one of yours. It's not just about what you accomplish this summer; it's about how these missions shape you and the world around you for years to come.

Consider this: The skills you sharpen, the alliances you forge, and the challenges you overcome won't just vanish like smoke after the summer fades. They're etching a new blueprint onto your character that will guide you in ways you might not expect. Today's volunteer gig could be the spark that ignites your passion for a future career or the experience that turns you into a lifelong advocate for a cause close to your heart.

Let's not forget the ripple effect. By stepping up and making a difference, you're setting an example that can inspire others to follow in your footsteps. It's like dropping a pebble into a pond—the ripples spread far and wide, touching shores you might never see. This summer, you're not just volunteering; you're planting seeds of change that will grow long after your initial effort.

As you reflect on your journey, consider how this summer's service can influence your future decisions, career paths, and personal growth. Each mission, each act of kindness, is a step toward becoming not just a hero for a summer but a hero for life.

So, as we sign off from this chapter of your adventure, remember: The impact of a single summer can echo through time, shaping your path and touching lives in ways you can't yet imagine. You have the power to make this summer a turning point, not just for those you help but for yourself. The question isn't if you'll leave a mark—it's what kind of mark you'll choose to leave.

Onward, agent of change, to a Summer of Service that will launch a lifetime of impact.

Chapter 11

Signing Off

As you gear up for your next adventure, remember that the world of volunteerism is vast, filled with mysteries waiting to be uncovered and lives waiting to be touched. Keep your gadgets close, your allies closer, and your heart open. Your mission, should you choose to accept it, is to continue making pearls of positive impact.

Embrace the unknown with the courage of a seasoned spy. Each step you take into new volunteering opportunities unlocks more than just personal achievement—it opens doors to new alliances, unveils the depth of human experience, and crafts a legacy of compassion and action. As you venture forward, carry the tools and tales from your past missions. Use them to navigate the challenges ahead and to chart courses that others might follow.

And remember, every small act of kindness and every courageous step in service is part of a larger story—a story where you are both the hero and the author. So, write a narrative that's bold, craft chapters that inspire, and create endings that leave the world a better place than you found it.

Until next time, change agent.

Stay daring, stay dashing, and above all, stay kind.

Mission Command, over and out.

Chapter 12
About the Authors

If you want to touch the past, touch a rock.

If you want to touch the present, touch a flower.

If you want to touch the future, touch a life.

– Author Unknown

Change Agent Dossier: Cole Bailey

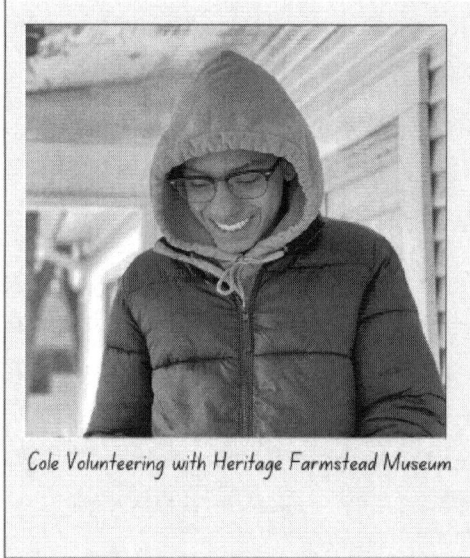

Cole Volunteering with Heritage Farmstead Museum

Code Name: Wildfire

Special Abilities:

Cole is energetic, determined, and a champion of the underdogs. He knows how to get people excited about a project and is really good at planning how to do it.

Background:

Talking is Cole's superpower. He can convince almost anyone of the merits of his ideas, and he's open to different viewpoints, making him an awe-some person to have around and to collaborate with.

Primary Skills:

Standing Up, Not Standing Out: Like many change agents, Cole stays out of the spotlight. He doesn't volunteer to get attention. He shies away from large crowds and blends in whenever possible. It's like hiding in plain sight at school or anywhere else.

Gourmet Guru: Cole loves exploring new foods and is known for his adventurous taste. He can tell you all about the best (and worst) foods at school and where to find the coolest food trucks. Following Cole on a food adventure means your lunch will never be boring!

Chameleon Curls: 'Fro today, fade tomorrow—his hairstyle shifts with the same ease and finesse as his plans. It's not just about looking good (though, let's be honest, it totally is); it's about making a statement. Cole's ever-changing hair symbol-izes his adaptability and willingness to embrace change, both in style and substance.

Weaknesses:

Honey Nut Cheerios Obsession: Cole's ability to power-talk and stand up for the underdog has an unusual fuel source: an insatiable appetite for Honey Nut Cheerios. This isn't just a breakfast routine; it's a full-blown obsession. Cole's daily intake of these honey-coated circles of goodness directly fuels his strategic thinking and persuasive abilities, but also might be a bit much.

Starbucks Stakeout Vulnerability: For Cole, Starbucks is more than a coffee haven; it's the critical source of his operational energy, making it the most predictable point in his daily routine. This love for the chain's signature brews has inadvertently turned every local Starbucks into a potential rendezvous point for counteragents. This predictable pattern could easily become his undoing, as foes could lie in wait, blending in with the morning rush, ready to intercept or eavesdrop on Wildfire.

Change Agent Dossier: Maddox Bailey

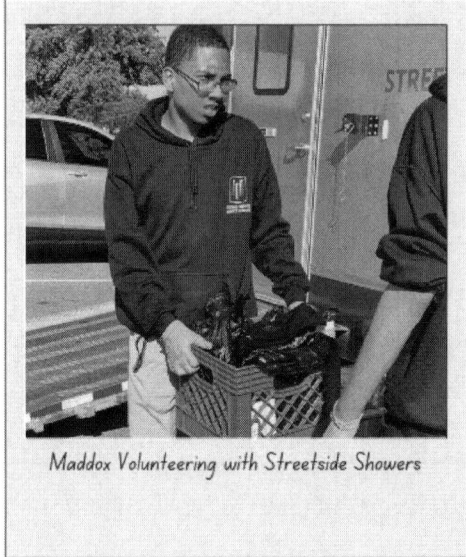

Maddox Volunteering with Streetside Showers

Code Name: Blizzard

Special Abilities:

He remains a cool, calm, and collected thinker in high-pressure situations.

Background:

A rare autoimmune disease attacked his brain and spinal cord, threatening to take him out, but he emerged victorious from this personal health battle. Maddox has proven that he's a survivor. This ordeal has sharpened his mind and reflexes, making him a formidable opponent in any arena he chooses to conquer.

Primary Skills:

- **Compassionate Companion:** Maddox strives to be a friend to the friendless and sees the good in everyone. He's always there with a listening ear or a comforting word, ensuring no one feels left out. His superpower is his ability to connect with others and make them feel valued.

- **Soccer Field Illusionist:** Maddox dominates on the soccer field with shifty moves and lightning speed. He has a natural ability to appear where opponents least expect him.

- **Chessboard Conqueror:** Off the field, Maddox's strategic mind shines brightest on the chessboard. His battles have taught him to think several moves ahead, making him an awe-inspiring strategist who can turn the tide of any game with a single, well-planned move.

Weaknesses:

- **Sweet Tooth Sabotage:** Despite his disciplined mind, Maddox's one vulnerability lies in his insatiable craving for Dr Pepper. This Achilles' heel is known to his adversaries, who realize that a well-placed soda can distract or delay him from his missions.

- **Lone Wolf Syndrome:** Maddox's inclination to shoulder the burden of group projects reflects his strong sense of responsibility. However, this tendency to take on all the work risks burnout and overlooks the value of team collaboration and delegation.

- **The Silent Strategist:** Maddox's quiet nature, while a strength on the chessboard and soccer field, sometimes acts as a barrier in more vocal environments. His reluctance to speak up can lead to missed opportunities to share his valuable insights, which this book will undoubtedly correct.

Chapter 13

Mission Control

ACKNOWLEDGMENTS

Every hero's journey is supported by an incredible crew, and the adventure that led to *Summer of Service* is no exception. We want to give a shout-out to the remarkable allies who've made this mission possible:

Heading off to the first day of school
The Shelton School, Dallas, TX

The Shelton School in Dallas, Texas – Cheers for the incredible educators at The Shelton School! You didn't just teach two boys with dyslexia how to read and write. You unlocked a world of potential and adventure. Thanks for turning challenges into triumphs and giving us the tools to tell this story.

Enrolling in Lovejoy ISD at the little red schoolhouse

English and Special Education Departments of Lovejoy ISD – We have so much love for the teachers, counselors, and dyslexia therapists. Your passion for language and patience for supporting kids who need extra help to learn has helped countless students, like us, to explore the power of storytelling.

Volunteering with Meals on Wheels

Young Men's Service League – A giant shout-out to the Young Men's Service League, especially the Plano Chapter, for fostering a spirit of community and love for volunteerism. Your commitment to service and leadership has not only shaped us to be good citizens but also empowered us to take action and make a real impact.

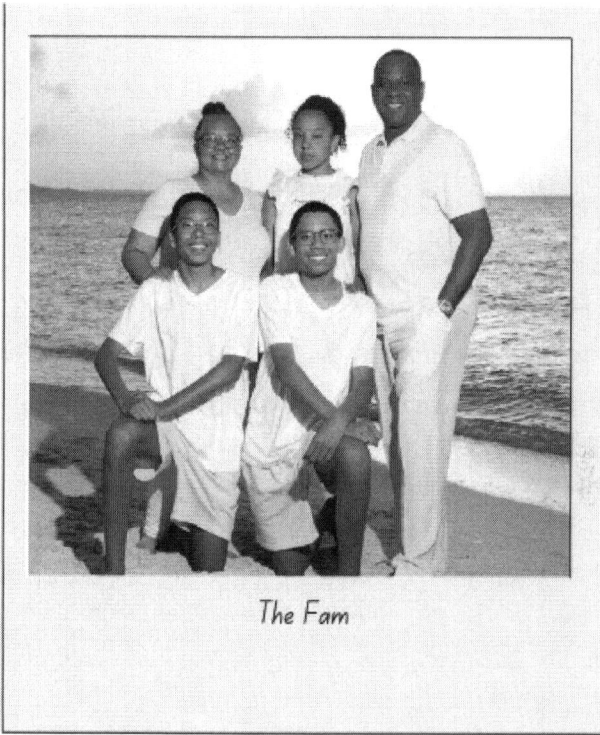

The Fam

Our Family: Mom, Dad, and Sheridan—To our personal cheer squad and the best support team a change agent could ask for, Mom and Dad, your endless encouragement and wisdom (and the money to pay for professional book editors) are how this book happened in the first place. It was definitely a team effort, even though our names are on the covers.

And to our little sister Sheridan, thank you for the laughs and for keeping us grounded as our unofficial hype queen. Your energy keeps us humble and real, always.

All of you played a pivotal role in this mission, providing the inspiration, support, and love that fueled the work. As we share this guide with fellow change agents looking to make a difference, we carry forward the lessons and values you've instilled in us.

Here's to making the world a better place, one summer mission at a time!

Made in the USA
Columbia, SC
03 June 2024

36241325R00067